Amazing Hands-On
Map Activities

by Rose Forina

SCHOLASTIC
PROFESSIONALBOOKS

New York • Toronto • London • Auckland • Sydney
Mexico City • New Delhi • Hong Kong • Buenos Aires

Acknowledgments

Amazing Hands-On Map Activities was made possible with the help of family, friends, and students. They have been my compass in finding my way to writing and publishing this book.

To Phyllis Dubina, Gail McCune, and Patricia Messina, who encouraged me to submit a book proposal

To Sarah Longhi at Scholastic Professional Books, who listened to and liked my ideas

To Diane Barsotti, Mary Connolly, Teresa Forina, and Carol Merola, for their suggestions and advice

To Ellen Nickerson, who forgave my overdue books

To Walter Huston, who provided a map rubric that spurred the creation of the one in this book

To Jessica Frattaroli, for her diligent work in creating the model map of Plymouth Village

To my volunteer crew of student cartographers: Cassandra Busbee, Sarah Carroll, Benjamin Carsley, Jenna Deeb, Anthony Desmond, Samantha Hamilton, Grady McCune, Sarah McNeff, Natalie Moskal, Stephanie Moskal, Steven Nalen, Emalie Novick, Samuel Roberts, Allyson Shifley, Jessica Smith, Maria Spinazzola, and Nicole Spinazzola, for all their time and effort

To all my past and present students at the N. E. Willis School, for the thousands of maps they have made over the years

Cover design by Jim Sarfati

Cover photographs by Donnelly Marks

Interior design by Melinda Belter

Interior photographs: pages 9, 10, 15, 21, 22, 30, and 34 by Donnelly Marks; pages 19, 22, and 29 by Color Wheel; pages 8, 13, 23, 27, and 28 by Shaun Flagg; and pages 26, 32, and 33 by Rose Forina

Continent outlines, page 16, by Jim McMahon

Credits: Explorer Biopoem activity (page 31) adapted from a workshop sponsored by Research for Better Teaching, Inc.

ISBN: 0-439-26278-X

Contents

Activities

Resources

Introduction

Dear Teacher,

As a classroom teacher for twelve years, I have taught American history, land regions of the United States, and now, ancient civilizations. Whether the topic was Paul Revere's ride, the resources of the American Midwest, or the beginning of agriculture in the Fertile Crescent, the tool I always found most effective was a map. Maps help tell a story. They provide a visual context for understanding human exploration, migration, and settlement. Often times my students made maps of their own, and from their maps I learned a valuable lesson: When students experience first hand what goes into making a map, they can better read, interpret, and analyze other maps. It is for this reason I have written this book.

Amazing Hands-On Map Activities is a geography activity book that focuses on the student as cartographer. It provides step-by-step directions that will help you and your students make a variety of maps with everyday materials. You'll learn how to use a balloon to create a globe, make salt dough and shape it into a relief map, and turn a shoe box into a cultural museum. Most of the activities can be adapted for whole group, small group, or individual work. Photographs of student work have been included to give examples of how to create the maps and use them in a classroom.

In addition to its primary focus—hands-on map activities—this book also provides exciting ways to incorporate geography in your language arts curriculum. Several activities contain writing extensions such as Geography Acrostics (page 19), Explorer Biopoems (page 31), and Postcards (page 23) that involve students in research, writing, and mapmaking. Each activity's Web Link or Book Link section features my students' favorite geography resources—the ones that support great research in my classroom. Finally, to help your students become landform experts, I've designed a "Landform-Terms Mini-Book" which can be reproduced for each student's reference (page 38).

To help you best meet your social studies curriculum objectives, the map activities in this book have been aligned to several of the National Geography Standards. (See page 5 for a complete list of these standards.) Each activity page highlights the standard (or standards) targeted by the main activity and the extension activities. Keeping these standards in mind will help you plan well-rounded social studies lessons.

I am very excited to share this book with you. I hope you and your students use the book to make many amazing maps in your classroom. Most important, I hope these map-making projects will foster a love of geography and a lifelong interest in discovering the world and learning about its people.

Sincerely,
Rose Forina

4

National Geography Standards

In 1994, national standards were published in response to a need to strengthen geography education in our country. Many states have since adopted a number or all of these 18 standards. These standards are not intended to be prescriptive mandates. They are meant to serve as guides to help students better understand the world and their place in it.

I have used these standards to make geography teaching and learning come alive in my classroom. The activities in this book encourage you to incorporate these standards in your planning and lessons.

1 *Understand how to use maps and other geographic representations, tools, and technologies to acquire, process, and report information from a spatial perspective.*

2 *Understand how to use mental maps to organize information about people, places, and environments in a spatial context.*

3 *Understand how to analyze the spatial organization of people, places, and environments on Earth's surface.*

4 *Understand the physical and human characteristics of places.*

5 *Understand that people create regions to interpret Earth's complexity.*

6 *Understand how culture and experience influence people's perceptions of places and regions.*

7 *Understand the physical processes that shape the patterns of Earth's surface.*

8 *Understand the characteristics and spatial distribution of ecosystems on Earth's surface.*

9 *Understand the characteristics, distribution, and migration of human population on Earth's surface.*

10 *Understand the characteristics, distribution, and complexity of Earth's cultural mosaics.*

11 *Understand the patterns and networks of economic interdependence on Earth's surface.*

12 *Understand the processes, patterns, and functions of human settlement.*

13 *Understand how the forces of cooperation and conflict among people influence the division and control of Earth's surface.*

14 *Understand how human actions modify the physical environment.*

15 *Understand how physical systems affect human systems.*

16 *Understand the changes that occur in the meaning, use, distribution, and importance of resources.*

17 *Understand how to apply geography to interpret the past.*

18 *Understand how to apply geography to interpret the present and plan for the future.*

For more information on these standards, go to *National Geographic*'s Web site at www.nationalgeographic.com. A special section called Xpeditions provides a detailed description of each standard as well as related grade-level lessons and activities.

12 Tips for Creating a Geography-Rich Classroom

How can you help students become geography experts? What can you do to help them develop their map-making skills? Here are 12 ideas that will support geography learning in your classroom all year long.

GEOGRAPHY CENTER: Create a classroom geography center. Include a variety of maps, globes, atlases, trade books, almanacs, magazines, travel brochures, and software.

POSTCARD FILE REFERENCE: Collect postcards. These inexpensive geography gems are great resources for maps and photos. File them in shoe boxes according to continent and country for easy reference.

STAMP SORT: Stamps are another great source of geographic information. Much can be learned about political leaders, historical events, and native wildlife from postage stamps. Sort the stamps according to state, region, country, and/or continent and mount them in an album.

MAKE IT REAL: Real objects/souvenirs make great visual aids in your geography lessons. A real cotton boll, a swatch of silk, and a stick of cinnamon can help students make stronger connections as they study places such as North Carolina, China, or Sri Lanka.

QUESTION OF THE DAY: Use maps regularly in your classroom. Daily geography and current events questions are two ways to get your students to look at maps. Plot geographic locations on a large map using map pins or adhesive notes.

MAP VOCAB: Model the use of correct geographic terms and refer to specific locations. Incorporating terms such as *strait* and *isthmus* in your instructions and discussions—during the mapmaking process and throughout the year—will foster geographic literacy in your classroom.

STUDENT MAP PRESENTATIONS: Provide opportunities for students to present their maps to others. Oral presentations are an excellent avenue for students to explain the process they used to create their maps.

TECHNOLOGY AND GEOGRAPHY: Incorporate technology in mapmaking. The Internet is a tremendous resource for geographic information and maps. Create a Webquest that focuses on maps. Compile student work into a PowerPoint classroom atlas or a Hyperstudio presentation. Publish students' maps on a classroom Web site.

PEN PALS AND E-PALS: Exchanging letters is a great way to share and learn about different places, traditions, and customs. Thanks to the Internet, classrooms can now enjoy digital correspondence with pen pals across the country or throughout the world. (See Web links, page 35.)

"MAPPING" A BOOK: If your class is involved in literature circles, add the role of mapmaker to appropriate book selections. This student is responsible for researching and providing geographic background as well as a map to the others in the circle.

EVALUATING PROGRESS: Use students' maps to assess learning before, during, or after a unit of study. Establish a rubric that lets your students know the assessment criteria. Students can use the rubric to self-evaluate their own maps and determine what they need to improve. (Use the rubric on page 37 as a model.)

MAP SYMBOLS AND ELEVATION SCALE: Encourage students to use standard map symbols and colors as they make their own maps. Regular use of these symbols will help them better read and interpret other maps. Enlarge the Map Symbols chart on page 7 and color in the elevation scale. Display it in your classroom for easy reference.

6

Map Symbols

national capital

state capital

other city ●

national boundary —— • —— • ——

state boundary – – – – –

oil drilling

ore mining

airport

state highway

interstate highway

railroad 〉〉〉〉〉〉

river ————

single mountain ▲

mountain range

compass rose N / W ◇ E / S

Elevation Scale

mountains	BROWN
highlands	ORANGE
plateaus	YELLOW
plains	GREEN
lowlands	DARK GREEN
water	BLUE

Mental Maps

Students' constructions of mental maps—maps drawn from memory—can provide a wealth of information about how students organize their understanding of a place. Use their mental maps as a part of your assessment of any social studies unit in pre- and post-performance tasks. In between assessments, you can use the following mental-mapping strategies to help students build their spatial organization skills and study the geography of a place.

My students' mental maps of the world, drawn in September and again later in the year, often show a tremendous improvement in accuracy, presentation, and use of map elements.

Before

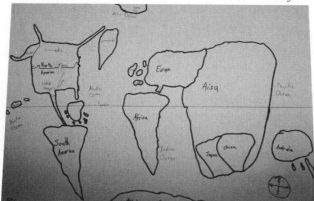

After

Book Link: Hartman, Gail. *As the Crow Flies: A First Book of Maps.* New York: Simon & Schuster, 1993. This easy reader serves as a primer to reading maps as land viewed from an aerial perspective. 📖

6 MENTAL-MAPPING STRATEGIES

- Associate the shape of actual map outlines with familiar objects (Italy looks like a heeled boot; Kentucky looks like a door key). Invite students to contribute their own imaginative associations.

- Ask students to close their eyes as you take them on an imaginary trip through the school or along a familiar route. Describe landmarks they encounter along the way. Can they draw an accurate route map afterward?

- Project a map on an overhead screen or use a large wall map and trace the map outline with a pointer or your finger. At the same time, have students follow along by drawing the map in the air. Be sure to use correct geographical terms.

- Provide students with string or yarn and have them shape the yarn to form the outline of a particular continent or country. Have them compare their yarn outlines with an actual map and make necessary adjustments.

- In making maps, students often need to see and present geographic information from an aerial view. Practice drawing objects such as apples and prisms looking downward instead of from the side.

- Give each student a large sheet of paper, a pencil, and a map. Have students sketch the map on their papers while holding the actual map at arm's length. Tell students to look only at the map (**not** at their work) until they have finished drawing. Invite them to place their map over the original and compare the outlines and features they've drawn.

TEACHING TIP

Provide students with opportunities to compare their mental maps with standard maps.

Geography Notebook

This year-long activity involves students in compiling their own set of hand-drawn maps. Their collection can be customized to meet your particular social studies curriculum. If you are studying American history, include route maps of early explorers, a political map of the 13 colonies, or a battle map of Gettysburg. If your focus is ancient civilizations, include maps of Mesopotamia, Egypt, China, Greece, and Rome. Geography Notebooks can become part of each student's portfolio. Use their maps and the rubric on page 37 to assess their mapmaking skills. At the end of the year, your students' atlases will be brimming with dozens of different kinds of maps, and you'll have a record of each student's progress.

NATIONAL GEOGRAPHY STANDARD 1

Understand how to use maps and other geographic representations, tools, and technologies to acquire, process, and report information from a spatial perspective.

Preparation

You'll need to plan what kinds of maps and what type of information you want your students to show. I type a list of captions that are then cut out and pasted in the map margins. An example of a caption is "Africa is the hottest continent in the world." When my students are going to draw this particular map, I also provide them with a list of required labels, such as the Isthmus of Suez, Atlas Mountains, Madagascar, Sahara Desert, Mt. Kilimanjaro, Atlantic Ocean, Indian Ocean, Nile River, Congo River, Mediterranean Sea, and Red Sea. Students are responsible for including these features in their maps (see student samples, page 10).

TEACHING TIP

Make color transparencies of your students' maps and use them in your lessons. Select and compile maps into a PowerPoint Atlas that can be shared with the rest of the school and parents. Kids love to see their work on the projector and computer screen!

WHAT TO GET

➤ reproducible cover, page 11
➤ construction paper
➤ paper fasteners
➤ vertical/horizontal map reproducible (for long or wide maps), page 12
➤ colored pencils or crayons
➤ three-hole puncher

WHAT TO DO

To make the cover:

1. Distribute copies of the Geography Notebook cover on page 11 and have students illustrate a cover for their atlas.
2. Mount the cover (or have them design their own cover) on a sheet of construction paper.
3. Laminate the front cover and a back page. (If a laminator is not available, students can keep their maps in a folder or binder.)
4. Punch holes in the front and back covers. Attach with paper fasteners.

To make the maps:

1. Make one copy of the map reproducible (page 12) placing a sticky note over the compass rose at bottom left for vertical (long) map or placing the sticky note over the compass rose at the bottom right for a horizontal (wide) map.
2. Cut and paste teacher-prepared caption in the outer margin.
3. Make copies for students and hole punch copies.
4. Provide a list of required labels by writing them on the blackboard or worksheet. (See sample list of labels on page 10.)

9

Sample of Labels and Student Work

Here are two samples of maps created by my fourth-grade students. The North American map is from a series of seven continent maps that were made during our geography review in September. The map of ancient Greece is part of our study of ancient civilizations.

NORTH AMERICA, required labels

Appalachian Mountains
Rocky Mountains
Mount McKinley
Arctic Ocean
Atlantic Ocean
Pacific Ocean
Mississippi River
Gulf of Mexico
Great Plains
Greenland
Cuba
West Indies

ANCIENT GREECE, required labels

Thebes
Crete
Olympia
Athens
Sparta
Delphi
Mycenae
Knossus
Corinth
Aegean Sea
Ionian Sea

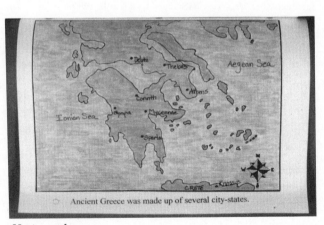

Ancient Greece was made up of several city-states.

Horizontal map

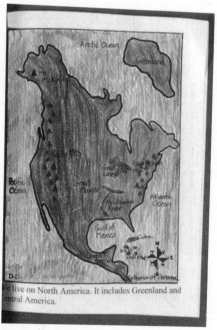

We live on North America. It includes Greenland and Central America.

Vertical map

Web Link: Geography http://www.geography.about.com
This Web site is an extensive geographic resource. Printable outline maps of the world, individual countries, and U.S. states are available for use in the classroom. Clicks on the navigation bar will lead you to great geography lesson plans, games, and much more. ☐

GEOGRAPHY
NOTEBOOK

NAME _____

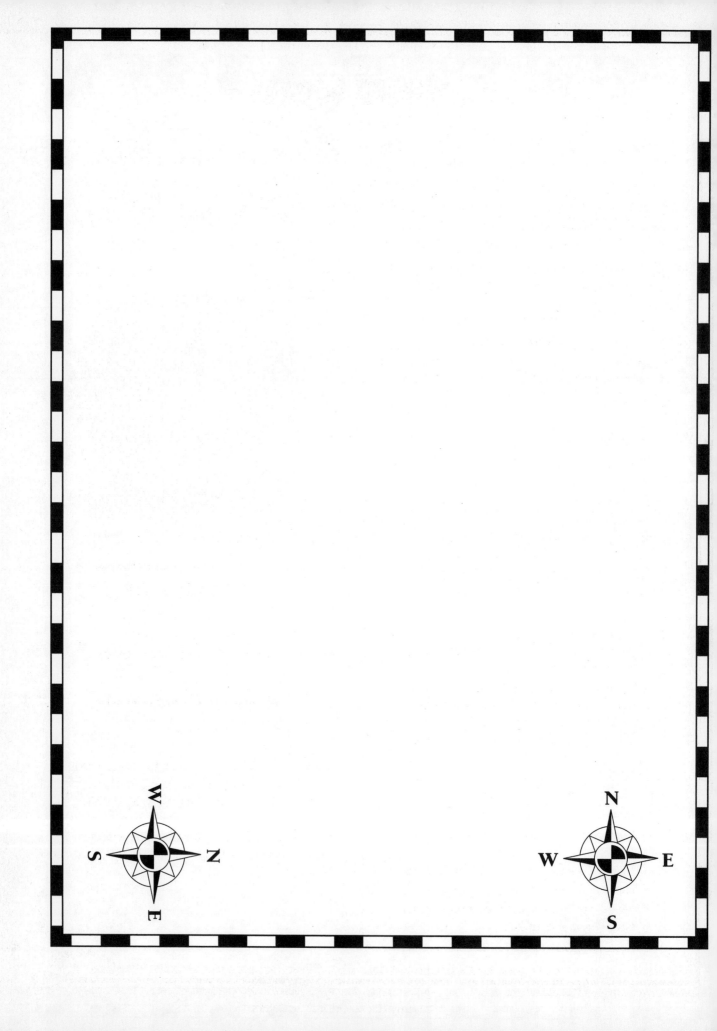

Gourd Globes

Turning a gourd into a globe can be a great geography lesson. The natural spherical shape of a pumpkin and its vertical indentations make it an optimal model to demonstrate circumference, hemispheres, poles, equator, and latitude and longitude. Students can measure the circumference of the pumpkin, the length from the stem to the base, and compare their findings with the actual dimensions of Earth.

NATIONAL GEOGRAPHY STANDARD 1

Understand how to use maps and other geographic representations, tools, and technologies to acquire, process, and report information from a spatial perspective.

WHAT TO GET

➤ pumpkins
➤ water-based markers
➤ string or yarn
➤ green acrylic paint
➤ continent outlines, page 16
➤ blue acrylic paint
➤ scissors
➤ brushes
➤ masking tape
➤ permanent markers

WHAT TO DO

1. Tape a length of string or yarn around the middle of the pumpkin. Trace along the string or yarn to mark the equator. This reference line will help students correctly position the continents.

2. Cut out continent outlines and tape them into place on the pumpkin. Note: Since pumpkins come in all sizes, you may need to enlarge or reduce the continent outlines.

3. Use water-based markers to trace the continent outlines. These markers make lines that can easily be wiped off and redrawn.

4. Draw major islands in freehand.

5. Paint the continents and islands green. Let the paint dry.

6. Paint the oceans, seas, and other water areas blue. Let the paint dry.

7. Retrace the outlines of the landmasses with black permanent marker.

TEACHING TIP

Provide globes and world maps for students to consult as they draw and paint their pumpkins.

Book Link: Lye, Keith, and Alistair Campbell. *Atlas in the Round: Our Planet as You've Never Seen It.* Philadelphia: Running Press, 1999. Share this book with your class prior to making a papier-mâché globe. Consult it in positioning and drawing the continents and islands.

Papier-Mâché Globes

Tear up lots and lots of newspaper, make a batch of starchy water, and watch your students transform party balloons into their own globes. The process takes about five 45-minute sessions. Use this work time and students' globes to teach them about the circumference of Earth, the northern and southern hemispheres, and other geography basics.

WHAT TO GET

- ➤ 9 inch round balloons (one per student)
- ➤ stapler
- ➤ continent outlines, page 16
- ➤ masking tape
- ➤ brushes
- ➤ green tempera paint
- ➤ plastic drop cloth/trash bags
- ➤ black permanent marker
- ➤ 4- by 18-inch poster board strips (one per student)
- ➤ large bowl (one per four students)
- ➤ newspaper
- ➤ water
- ➤ liquid starch
- ➤ measuring cup
- ➤ blue tempera paint

WHAT TO DO

To make the sphere:

1. Tear newspaper into 1- by 3-inch strips. You'll need many, many strips so you might want to do this step a day ahead.
2. Cover your work area with a plastic drop cloth. Trash bags work fine, too.
3. In a bowl, prepare a solution of 3 cups starch and 1 cup water for every four students.
4. Bend the poster board strip into a circle and staple it together at the ends. This will be the base on which the balloon globe will rest. Label the base with student's name.
5. Inflate balloons to 9 inches. Be careful not to inflate the balloons too much or they will look like eggs rather than spheres. Also, try to keep size of balloons consistent at 9 inches to avoid making the size of the cutout continents disproportionate to the area of water surrounding them. Knot the balloons and place them on the base.
6. Dip one strip of newspaper at a time into the solution and place it onto the balloon. Be sure to overlap the strips and smooth the edges to avoid buckling. Do not cover the balloon knot.
7. Continue applying the wet newspaper strips until the balloon is completely covered. Let it dry overnight.
8. Repeat steps 6–7 two more times.
9. Tug at the balloon knot and cut with scissors. (Students enjoy hearing the crackling sound as the inside balloon pulls away from the paper shell.)
10. Patch the hole with a small strip of newspaper dipped in the papier-mâché solution. Let it dry for about an hour.

Continued on following page

14

WHAT TO DO

To draw the map:

1. Make copies of and cut out the continent outlines from page 16.

2. Draw a line around the middle of the balloon. This equator will help students place the continents in their proper locations.

3. Tape the continent cutouts in place and use them as guides to trace around with a marker. This step may prove challenging for students: tracing flat continents onto a sphere often distorts these landmasses—a geography lesson in itself! Students may need to draw in freehand parts of continents. Have globes readily available for students to consult as they draw their continents.

4. Use a marker to sketch in major islands.

5. Paint the landmasses with the green paint. Let the paint dry.

6. Paint the bodies of water blue. Again, let the paint dry.

7. Outline the continents and islands in marker.

TEACHING TIP

A suggested tracing order is Antarctica, then South America, North America, Africa, Eurasia, and finally Australia.

Book Link: Lye, Keith, and Alistair Campbell. *Atlas in the Round: Our Planet as You've Never Seen It.* Philadelphia: Running Press, 1999. Share this book with your class prior to making a papier-mâché globe. Consult it in positioning and drawing the continents and islands. 📖

CONTINENT OUTLINES

Use these outlines as a guide when you draw the continents for the gourd globe or papier-mâché globe.

- **Outlines help you position the continents:** You can cut out and tape these outlines onto your globe. Check their positions by comparing them to a standard globe and move them, if necessary.
- **Size and shape distortions:** Are these flat outlines the correct shape when you place them on the curved surface of the globe? Nope. You'll need to stretch them out a bit! As you trace around these outlines on your globe, adjust the size and shape of the landmasses to fit correctly on your globe. Use a standard globe to guide you.
- **Missing islands:** Where's Japan? A lot of land is missing from these continents! On your globe be sure to draw in the major island groups that are not included below. Again, use a standard globe to guide you.

Scaled Room Maps

"How can we get our classroom to fit on this piece of paper?" This question is a great opener to a lesson that will result in making a scaled map of the classroom. It will involve students in measuring, collecting, and recording data, calculating a scale ratio, and making a map.

WHAT TO GET

➤ metersticks, yardsticks, or measuring tape

➤ ruler

➤ grid paper

➤ colored pencils or colored paper

➤ markers

WHAT TO DO

1. Draw a rough sketch of the classroom. Mark the location of doors, windows, chalkboards, and so on. Include the placement of desks, bookcases, worktables, and computer stations. (Set reasonable expectations about how much detail to include.)

2. Measure and record the length and width of the room, the distances from one item to another, and the dimensions of the pieces of furniture that will be featured. (To make this task simpler and to encourage students to use estimation skills, round all measurements to the nearest foot.)

3. Calculate the scale ratio to be used. (1 grid square = 1 square foot works well for us.)

4. Count out the necessary squares on grid paper to mark out the perimeter of the room. Use a ruler to draw it on the grid paper.

5. Determine the location and number of squares needed for doors, windows, chalkboards, and furniture. Use a ruler to mark them on the grid paper. Color the squares or cut colored paper to size and glue the cutouts onto the marked spaces. (Using different colors to group similar items—class library, student desks, learning centers, and so on—can help increase students' abilities to visually organize the room.)

6. Label the different places on the map.

7. Include a map scale.

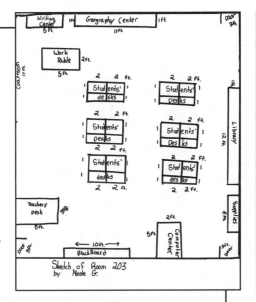

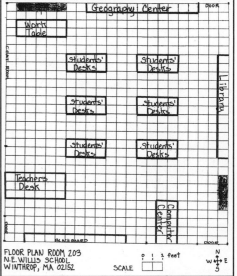

Book Link: Leedy, Loreen. *Mapping Penny's World.* New York: Holt, 2000. This picture book is a great introduction to mapmaking. When Lisa is given a homework assignment to make a map, she creates a variety of maps—from a floor plan of her bedroom to a map of the world. Readers will learn the importance of map features—such as symbols, scale, and the compass rose—in all the maps Lisa makes.

TEACHING TIP

As a home assignment, students can measure and make scaled drawings of their bedroom, kitchen, or living room.

Mural Maps

Does your class need a large map of the world, the United States, or a particular area you are studying? Well, roll up your sleeves, cover a large area with mural paper, and make your own map. Creating a classroom mural map will involve your students in a cooperative team effort, strengthen their map skills, and produce a project they will be proud to call their own.

In September my class begins the school year by making a 10-foot by 4-foot mural map of the world, and each student chooses to learn about a different location depicted on the map.

TEACHING TIP

Use a restickable adhesive glue stick (such as Post-it or Scotch brand) to customize your map with arrows, photos, and/or magazine cutouts. This special adhesive makes it easy to add and remove labels for a specific lesson or unit without damaging the map.

WHAT TO GET

- map transparency
- overhead projector
- permanent markers (blue and black, thick and fine points)
- blue tempera paint
- sponge sticks
- mural paper
- pencil
- green tempera paint
- cotton swabs
- tape

WHAT TO DO

1. Make a transparency of the map you want to enlarge.
2. Tape mural paper onto a large wall.
3. Cast an image of the map transparency on the mural paper using an overhead projector. Adjust the image to the size you need. Trace the outline of the map with pencil.
4. Use sponge sticks and green tempera to paint the land areas. Use cotton swabs to get into small and difficult areas. Let dry overnight.
5. Apply blue paint to the bodies of water. Use cotton swabs for small areas. Let dry overnight.
6. Retrace the borders with thick black permanent marker.
7. Draw rivers with blue permanent marker.
8. Label locations with fine-point black permanent marker.
9. Include a compass rose.

Mural Maps, continued

WRITING EXTENSION: Geography Acrostic

Use the mural map as a springboard for research and poetry writing. Have students focus on a particular place they would like to study. After taking notes from books and Internet resources, students synthesize information in the form of an acrostic poem. This format uses the first letter of each line to spell out the topic word when read vertically. Students can accompany the poem with a hand-drawn map of the location. They can also design a map border to illustrate a particular line from the poem.

WRITING EXTENSION: ABC Book

Making a mural map of a particular country can inspire mini-writing assignments that culminate in publishing a classroom ABC book. Current children's literature abounds with nonfiction books that present information in ABC format. Use these books as models, and have your class write their own ABC book on a particular geographic location. Assign letters of the alphabet to groups of children and provide time for research and writing (use reproducible template, page 20). Both the mural map and the ABC book serve as a great way to learn and review important geographic information.

My class was very fortunate to be E-pals with students from Queensland, Australia. Our correspondence got us curious about this interesting and faraway country. Writing our class book, *Australia A to Z*, was a fun and easy way to learn about Australia's geography, history, and culture.

Book Link: *National Geographic World Atlas for Young Explorers*. Washington, D.C.: National Geographic Society, 1998. 📖

Web Link: MegaMaps
http://www.yourchildlearns.com/megamaps.htm
Have plenty of paper in your printer to make large maps of the United States or the world. ☐

G laciers cover this arctic land.
R eindeer roam the permafrost.
E verywhere is mostly mountain and ice.
E xports fish and shrimp.
N uuk is its capital.
L ots of icebergs circle the icy coast.
A long the coast hunters search for seals in kayaks.
N ortheast of North America is this largest island.
D enmark is its mother country.

By Julia

E lk is a large deer that roams the northern tundra.
U nited Kingdom is part of the British Isles.
R ed and green grapes are pressed into fine wine.
O ld masters' paintings hang in the Louvre and other museums.
P opulation here is decreasing.
E uropean brown bear is one of the largest bears in the world.

By Bryan

A rt and music are popular.
F irst humans lived on this continent.
R hinos, zebras, and giraffes roam the grassy savanna.
I t has the biggest desert called the Sahara.
C ongo Basin has lots of rain.
A pes, monkeys, and birds live in the hot jungle.

By Matt

S is for sheep. There are more sheep than people in Australia. The sheep are raised on places called stations. There are over 105,000 sheep stations in Australia, and the sheep are used for their milk, meat, and especially their wool. At the stations the sheep are sheared, and the wool is cleaned, combed and sent to all parts of the world. Australian wool, especially from Merino sheep, is very fine quality wool.

GEOGRAPHY ABCs

Use this ABC chart to help you keep an alphabetical list of the facts you research and learn about your location.

A	
B	
C	
D	
E	
F	
G	
H	
I	
J	
K	
L	
M	
N	
O	
P	
Q	
R	
S	
T	
U	
V	
W	
X	
Y	
Z	

Floor Maps

The inspiration for this floor map came from a field trip to the Museum of Fine Arts in Boston. On the floor of their Ancient Near East Wing is a large stone map of the ancient Mediterranean world. My fourth graders sat around the map as they discussed the places we had read about in class—the Mediterranean and Red seas, the Tigris and Euphrates rivers, Mesopotamia and Sumer. We thought, "Wouldn't it be great to enjoy such maps back at school?" Here's what we did to create a floor map of China.

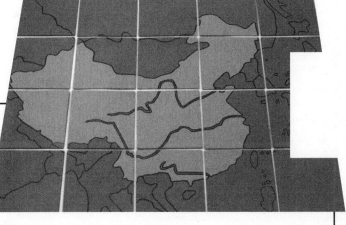

WHAT TO GET

➤ twenty 10- by 10-inch squares (wood, linoleum, or poster board)
➤ pencil
➤ permanent marker
➤ mural paper
➤ masking tape
➤ scissors
➤ acrylic paints
➤ map transparency
➤ brushes
➤ overhead projector
➤ Optional: acrylic spray or polyurethane (teacher-use only)

WHAT TO DO

1. Arrange the squares into a rectangle.
2. Measure and cut mural paper to cover the area of the squares.
3. Tape the paper to a wall.
4. Project the map transparency onto the wall. Adjust the image to fit the paper.
5. Trace the map outline and locations with pencil. Then copy over with permanent marker.

Continued on following page

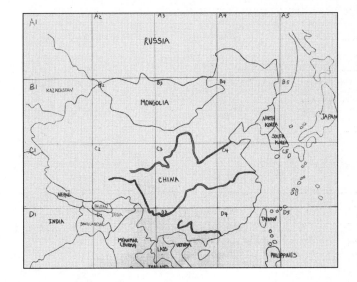

6. On the reverse side of the traced map, use a pencil to shade heavily over marker lines. This shading provides plenty of residue for transferring the traced map onto the tile squares.

7. Place the traced map onto the squares (the marker side should be faceup and the shaded pencil side should be facedown). Tape the map down to secure it in place. Retrace the map onto the squares, leaving a graphite tracing of the original map on the squares.

8. Retape the map to the wall. Measure and divide the map into twenty 10- by-10-inch sections. Label each square area A1, A2, B3, and so on. Refer to this map during the rest of the activity.

9. Assign each student or pair of students a map square. Label the back of each square A1, A2, B3, and so on, corresponding to sections on the map.

10. Paint the land and water areas of the map squares using acrylic paints. Let the paint dry.

11. Assemble all squares. Touch up and make adjustments if necessary. Let the paint dry.

12. Outline land areas of the map squares and label important places with permanent marker.

13. **(teacher only)** In a well-ventilated area, away from students, apply one or two coats of water-based polyurethane or acrylic spray to wood or linoleum squares for durability. If you used poster-board squares, laminate them.

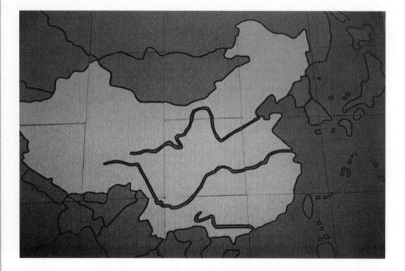

TEACHING TIP

Scramble the squares to create a puzzle. Have students manipulate and rearrange the sections to make the map.

Web Link: MegaMaps
http://www.yourchildlearns.com/megamaps.htm
Stock your printer with plenty of paper to make large maps of the United States or the world. ☐

Rubber-Stamp Maps

Using outlines of continents, countries, or states, students can have fun making rubber stamps of such places as Australia, India, or Massachusetts. Include labels on the "stamped" maps to mark rivers, mountains, and major cities. Use the stamps to decorate report covers, make postcards (see extension activity below) and note cards, or to create borders for bulletin boards.

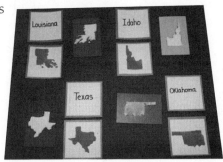

WHAT TO GET

➤ map outlines

➤ printing ink/tempera paint (see tip)

➤ foam sheets (see tip)   ➤ paper plate

➤ scissors   ➤ brayer

➤ glue   ➤ paper

➤ sturdy bases (wood, plexiglass, plastic, or cardboard)

WHAT TO DO

1. Cut out the desired map outline.
2. Trace the outline onto the foam sheet.
3. Cut the foam sheet along the traced lines.
4. Spread glue on the front side of the cut foam. Place it glued side down onto the base. Let it dry.
5. Pour ink or paint onto a paper plate.
6. Roll the brayer in the ink and then onto the foam stamp. Be sure to cover the entire surface of the stamp.
7. Press the stamp onto paper.

TEACHING TIP

Foam sheets are easy to cut and are available at most craft stores. If a visit to the craft store is not in your plan, recycled styrofoam trays from the school cafeteria work well, too. Large ink pads can be used instead of brayers and paint.

WRITING EXTENSION: Postcards

Student-made postcards offer an effective way to integrate geography and writing. Have students use the rubber stamps they've made to design the face of a postcard. After researching the particular continent, country, or state, students can weave information about geography, history, and culture into a note on the back of the postcard to send to a relative or friend. They can also detail some of this information by designing a postage stamp for their postcard and illustrating it with local wildlife, famous people, or historical events. (Have sample postcards available for students to use as models: See Book and Web Links for sources.) The student-made postcards can be compiled and published in a classroom book for reference—and a good read!

Book and Web Links: Williams, Vera B. *Stringbean's Trip to the Shining Sea.* New York: Scholastic, 1989. This book and the Web site Postcards From America (http://postcardsfrom.com/) provide excellent formats for students to use in creating and writing their own postcards. 📖 ▢

Web Link: States and Capitals http://50states.com/

If you are making rubber-stamp maps of the 50 states, this site will provide excellent templates for your students to use. Click on to any of the state buttons, scroll down the list of available information, and click on to maps. The black-and-white outline maps can be printed out and used for this activity. ▢

POSTCARD TEMPLATE

PLACE
STAMP
HERE

Postcard

ADDRESS

Overlay Maps

Creating an overlay map offers an excellent opportunity to make two maps in one. As students draw and label both a political and physical map of the same location, they will be able to compare and contrast the different types of information presented.

Map of Asia with overlay

Map of Asia

WHAT TO GET

➤ reference maps (physical and political)
➤ clear vinyl sheeting (see tip)
➤ poster board
➤ scissors
➤ paper clips
➤ stapler
➤ acrylic or poster paints
➤ permanent or water-based markers
➤ brushes

WHAT TO DO

1. Measure and cut the vinyl sheeting to the same size as the poster board.

2. Draw an outline of the location onto the poster board.

3. Place the vinyl sheeting over the poster board. Secure it in place using paper clips. Trace the outline onto the vinyl sheeting with permanent markers. Put the vinyl-sheeting cover aside.

4. Consult a physical map and color the poster board using different colors to represent various elevations. (See page 7 for standard elevation colors.)

5. Consult a political map and label the vinyl-sheeting cover with major cities, points of interest, and/or boundaries. Depending on your purpose, labels can be made using either permanent or water-based markers. Water-based markers will allow students to erase and reuse the map.

6. Place the vinyl-sheeting cover over the poster board and staple it in place at the top.

7. Fold a rectangular strip of poster board over the stapled top of the two maps. Glue it into place. Use the strip to give a title to your overlay map.

TEACHING TIPS

• Clear vinyl sheeting is inexpensive and is available in rolls at most fabric stores. You can also use a transparent shower curtain.

• Students can make their own 8-1/2- by 11-inch overlay maps with drawing paper and transparency sheets used for the overhead projector.

Web Link: Atlapedia Online
http://www.atlapedia.com/index.html
This site's World Maps section provides both physical and political maps of the same location. Have students refer to this site in planning their overlay map. ☐

Puzzle Maps

Do your students need to identify and locate the 50 U.S. states or the countries of Europe or Africa? Combine their skill at mapmaking and their love of games to make jigsaw puzzle maps. Sorting and putting the pieces together helps students identify states, countries, and continents. What better way to learn political and geographic boundaries!

WHAT TO GET

- poster board
- masking tape
- map transparency
- overhead projector
- pencil
- plastic bag/storage box
- permanent marker
- crayons/colored pencils
- laminator
- scissors

WHAT TO DO

1. Tape poster board onto a wall.
2. Project the map transparency on to the poster board using an overhead projector. Trace the outline and boundaries in pencil and then in permanent marker.
3. Color and label your map.
4. Laminate the map.
5. Cut the laminated map into pieces. (Follow boundary lines if you would like a political puzzle map. Cut surrounding bodies of water or neighboring landmasses into jigsaw pieces.)
6. Label and number the reverse side of the pieces using a permanent marker.
7. Store the pieces in plastic bags labeled with the appropriate map title. Identifying each set of map pieces is especially important when you create more than one set of puzzle maps.

Book Link: Keller, Laurie. *The Scrambled States of America.* New York: Holt, 1998. When the Midwest state of Kansas gets bored, it throws a party at which all the states get scrambled into different positions. This humorous book serves up a great geography lesson about the fifty states, their shapes, statistics, and position in the continental United States. 📖

Web Link: Maps.com
http://maps.com/
How well do you know your US geography? In the Learn and Play section, click onto map games and put together a jigsaw puzzle of the USA. Keep score as you drag and drop states into position. ☐

TEACHING TIP

Add Velcro® or magnetic strips to the reverse side of the puzzle pieces for use on a flannel board or magnetic board.

26

Grid Maps

Grid maps are made using the straight lines of graph paper. The simplified shapes that result will help students visualize the outlines of different countries as well as their locations in particular continents. Making grid maps will also give them a chance to compare the relative areas of different places.

WHAT TO GET

➤ copies of political maps
➤ tracing or butcher paper
➤ graph paper
➤ pencil
➤ black permanent marker
➤ colored pencils, markers, or crayons

TEACHING TIP

Integrate this map activity with a math lesson. Have students estimate how many square units will be covered by a particular country or region. Students can then calculate the number of squares covered by a particular country, order the countries from greatest area to least, and compare their results with the actual area of these places.

WHAT TO DO

1. Use a black marker to trace the outlines of a political map onto tracing paper. Be sure to make your lines thick enough to be easily seen.
2. Place the tracing under the graph paper. Retrace the outline and political borders onto the graph paper using a pencil.
3. Redraw the political boundaries with a black marker using **only** the grid lines of the graph paper. Follow the grid lines that are closest to the outline. Consult the political map to decide which lines to use.
4. Erase the pencil lines from around the grid map.
5. Color the grid map with colored pencils, markers, or crayons. Use a different color for each country or region.
6. Create a color-coded legend with countries' names.
7. Design a compass rose.

Web Link: National Geographic http://www.nationalgeographic.com
Print out all the political maps you need! The National Geographic Society encourages educators to use their maps in the classroom. Their Xpeditions Atlas offers more than 1,800 black-and-white maps that can be printed out in GIF or PDF format. ☐

Web Link: Geography http://www.geography.about.com
This geography site lists many, many links that can provide you with blank outline maps. Print out the maps you need and duplicate/enlarge them for your students to use in making their grid maps. ☐

Salt-Dough Relief Maps

Salt dough, or baker's clay, is an excellent medium for creating physical relief maps. Students can easily mold and shape the dough into form landforms such as mountains, plateaus, river valleys, and deltas. Once the dough dries completely, students can paint the map with poster paints, acrylics, and/or watercolors.

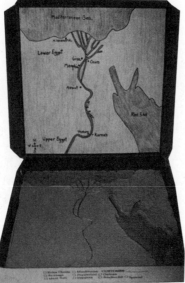

A pizza box makes an excellent display case for a salt-dough map. My students formed a relief map of ancient Egypt in the base of the box. Then, on drawing paper cut to the size of the cover, they designed a political map that showed the major cities along the Nile. They glued this map to the inside of the cover to offer two different geographic views of the same area.

WRITING EXTENSION: Fantasy Island

Don't throw away that extra salt dough! Invite students to knead and shape surplus salt dough to create a fantasy island. After consulting maps and globes, students decide where they would like to create a fictional island of their very own. The written component requires students to explain their island's relative location, topography, climate, and other features. An accompanying relief map can detail specific places mentioned in the writing.

Web Link: Atlapedia Online
http://www.atlapedia.com/index.html
Full color physical maps can be printed out for students to consult as they form their physical map using salt dough. ☐

WHAT TO GET

- large saucepan
- rolling pin
- plastic utensils
- 1 cup flour
- 1 tablespoon vegetable oil
- 2 teaspoons cream of tartar
- plastic container or bag
- heavy cardboard base
- measuring cups
- wooden spoon
- 1 cup water
- 1/2 cup salt
- paints
- brushes
- topographical map
- map pins (optional)

WHAT TO DO

To make the salt dough:

1. Measure and mix flour, oil, water, salt, and cream of tartar in the saucepan. (Add food coloring to the water to make a consistent dough color.)
2. Use a wooden spoon and stir over medium heat until the mixture comes together.
3. Knead the ball of dough until it has an elastic consistency.
4. Store in a covered container or plastic bag until you are ready to make the map.

To make the physical relief map:

1. Roll out enough dough to cover the cardboard base.
2. Consult a topographical map and mark the basic outline of the map using a plastic utensil. Add more dough for elevated areas. Use plastic utensils to carve and form landforms such as valleys, deltas, and river beds.
3. Insert map pins to mark particular locations (optional).
4. Let the map dry for about one week.
5. Paint the surface.

28

Landform Lids

Butte. Isthmus. Mesa. Plateau. Are you looking for a simple and easy way to teach your students about these and other landforms? This project helps students identify and understand the various physical features that make up Earth as they shape dough to re-create these features. Assign one or two different landforms to each student. This activity provides a tactile, three-dimensional complement to the Landform Terms Mini-Book on page 38.

This is the landform list my students choose from: archipelago, atoll, badlands, bay, butte, canyon, cape, cascade, cataract, cave, cliff, cove, delta, dune, fjord, glacier, gulf, hill, island, isthmus, key, lake, marsh, mesa, mountain, mouth, palisade, pampas, pass, peninsula, piedmont, plains, plateau, strait, tributary, valley, and volcano.

NATIONAL GEOGRAPHY STANDARD 7

Understand the physical processes that shape the patterns of Earth's surface.

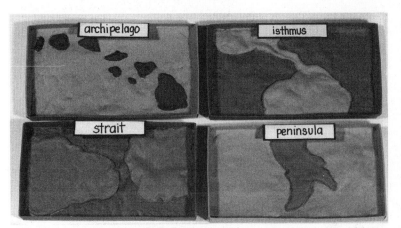

TEACHING TIP

Landform lids can also be displayed as plaques on a bulletin board. Before the dough dries, bore a hole in both the upper right and left corners of the lid. After the painted landform has dried, string a cord through the holes and display the plaque on the wall.

Book Link: Knowlton, Jack. *Geography A to Z*. New York: Thomas Y. Crowell, 1988. This illustrated glossary offers a great introduction to the major landforms that make up Earth. Each entry is beautifully illustrated, and the accompanying definition is clear and concise.

Web Link: Enchanted Learning—Geography http://www.enchantedlearning.com/geography/ The illustrated glossary of landforms and bodies of water provides a great reference for landform lids.

WHAT TO GET

➤ photos or illustrations of different landforms
➤ shoe box lids
➤ salt-dough recipe, page 28
➤ rolling pin
➤ poster paints, acrylics, or watercolors
➤ brushes
➤ cord (optional)

WHAT TO DO

1. Double the basic salt-dough recipe for each student.
2. Assign different landforms to your students (sample list at left). Provide photos and/or illustrations for them to refer to during the project.
3. Using a shoe box lid as the base, shape the dough into a particular landform. (See tip to find out how to create a hanging plaque.)
4. Let it dry for a week.
5. Paint the landform using poster paints, acrylics, or watercolors.
6. Let the paint dry overnight.

Tea-Stained Route Maps

Students will love getting their hands wet as they soak and stain their route maps with tea. Treasure and exploration maps that show the travels of Marco Polo, Columbus's voyages to the Americas, or the terrain of the Oregon Trail will look like they were drawn ages ago.

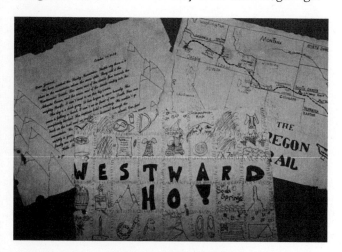

TEACHING TIP

Before applying the tea, make copies of the hand-drawn maps. During this process the paper gets very wet and might rip. If this happens, replace the torn map with another copy and repeat steps 2–5.

WRITING EXTENSION: Travel Journal

Students practice note-taking, letter-writing, and map-making skills in this travel journal project. Various stops along a journey are recorded as diary entries and marked on a route map. For example, in studying the Oregon Trail, my students took on the roles of various travelers in an 1860 wagon train—wagon master, travel guide, cook, teacher. They wrote diary entries in the first person and illustrated their work. Then they created a route map of the Oregon Trail, and stained all the pages with a concentrated brew of tea. Our class book *Westward Ho!* looked like it fell off a Conestoga wagon!

WHAT TO GET

- ➤ Copier-quality paper
- ➤ pencils
- ➤ permanent markers
- ➤ sponges (cut into pieces)
- ➤ rimmed cookie sheet/pan
- ➤ cord or ribbon (optional)
- ➤ tea bags
- ➤ water
- ➤ paper towels
- ➤ large bowl

WHAT TO DO

To make the map:

1. Use a pencil to draw the map on the paper.
2. Include labels, route arrows, compass rose, legend, and title.
3. Retrace markings with thin permanent marker.
4. Erase all pencil marks.

To stain the map:

1. Brew a very concentrated solution of tea. For every four students, brew about five bags of tea per cup of hot water. Let the mixture cool in a large bowl so that children can safely use it. Be sure to remove the tea bags before students begin working to avoid breaking the bags.
2. Place the map in the rimmed cookie sheet or pan.
3. Sponge the front of the map with the tea, making sure that the paper is completely covered with the tea.
4. Gently turn over the map. Repeat step 3.
5. Let the map dry on a surface covered with paper towels.
6. Roll the map and tie it with cord or ribbon (optional).

30

WRITING EXTENSION: Explorer Biopoem

After reading a biography of a famous explorer, students write an 11-line biopoem. This simple and adaptable format encourages students to truly analyze and synthesize the information about their subject. Students then design a cover and draw a route map of the journey. Follow the directions in making tea-stained maps to create an aged look for the cover, biopoem, and route map. Bind together with twine or leather strips.

1st line: First name

2nd line: Four descriptors (nouns, adjectives, or verbs)

3rd line: Relative of (son, daughter, husband, wife) _____

4th line: Who felt _____ (three emotions)

5th line: Who searched for _____ (three things and/or places)

6th line: Who needed _____ (three needs)

7th line: Who feared _____ (three fears)

8th line: Who gave _____ (three contributions)

9th line: Who found _____ (three things/places)

10th line: Resident of _____

11th line: Last name

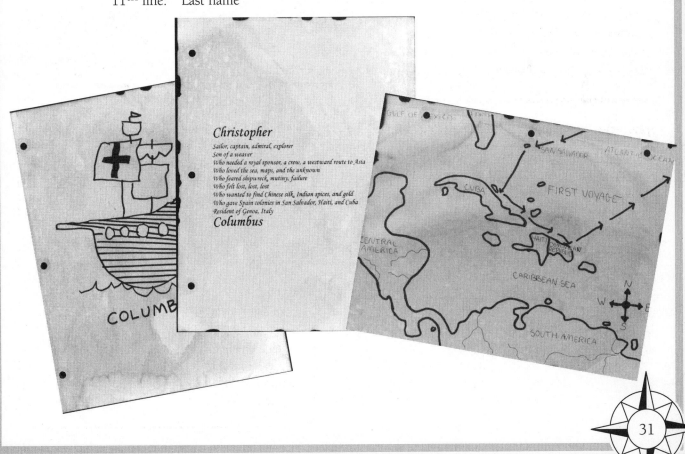

3-D Resource Maps

Resource maps are great tools to teach students about the natural resources, agriculture, and manufacturing of the world. Students can learn a great deal about the economy, trade, and culture of different countries by reading and making resource maps. As students plan their 3-D maps and design their map legends, they will discover the importance of symbols. Using actual objects for these symbols will appeal to your tactile learners and tap into children's love of collecting.

WHAT TO GET

➤ poster board
➤ crayons, colored pencils, paints, or markers
➤ glue
➤ various objects to represent resources, agriculture, or manufactured goods (e.g., painted pebbles for gold or silver, twigs for timber)

WHAT TO DO

1. Select a continent, country, or other region to research.
2. Draw an outline of the map of this place on posterboard. (See directions for mural maps steps 1–3, page 18.)
3. Color and label the map.
4. Design a map key that lists each of the resources or goods to be featured on this map. Leave adequate space to show the symbol.
5. Glue objects to the appropriate spaces in the key and on the map.
6. Include a title and compass rose.

TEACHING TIP

3-D resource maps are great visual aids for oral presentations. Ask students to explain their maps and the process involved in making them. Encourage them to bring in actual resources or products from the area they've studied (e.g., corn kernels to represent crops of corn in Russia), if those items are available.

Book Link: Priceman, Marjorie. *How to Make An Apple Pie and See the World.* New York: Dragonfly Books, 1994. When the local store is closed, a young girl sets out on a global journey in search of the ingredients needed to make an apple pie. As she collects semolina wheat from Italy, eggs from a French hen, and cinnamon from Sri Lanka, readers learn that food is grown, milled, and harvested from all parts of the world. The world map on the endpapers, a recipe for apple pie, and an intriguing ending all combine to make this book a classroom treasure.

Model Maps

Model maps are an effective way to develop spatial organization skills as students construct models of the local community, a colonial village, or even the ancient city of Pompeii. Encourage students to be creative in using all kinds of materials. We made the houses of our Pilgrim Village from lunch milk cartons, the clapboards from cut and painted wooden coffee stirrers, and thatched roofs from bundled pine needles.

TEACHING TIP

Schedule plenty of time with your students to brainstorm, sketch, and discuss ideas before they build the model. The cooperative experience, the geography learning, and the final product are well worth the time you'll invest.

WHAT TO GET

➤ reference map
➤ sturdy base
➤ masking tape
➤ paint
➤ construction paper
➤ tissue paper
➤ glue

Suggested building supplies:

➤ milk cartons (buildings)
➤ wooden blocks (buildings)
➤ cereal and shoe boxes (buildings)
➤ sand (landscape)
➤ twigs (landscape)
➤ gravel (landscape)
➤ mulch (landscape)
➤ any appropriate materials you can salvage from a recycling center

WHAT TO DO

1. Distribute a copy of the map to be made into a model. Consult the map regularly.
2. Sketch the map on the base. Use masking tape to section off areas. Mark the locations of natural features such as rivers, beaches, and forests. Lay out and label sites of human-made structures. (Discuss ways to depict relative sizes and proportions of buildings and/or landmarks—How large should the meetinghouse be in comparison to the blacksmith's shop? How could we show that?)
3. Brainstorm a variety of materials that can be used to depict natural and human-made features—and be sure to make use of recycled materials!
4. Construct models of houses and buildings using milk cartons, blocks, and other materials. Paint or cover them with construction or tissue paper. Add details to show structure and function.
5. Position the models on the map base.
6. Add landscape features using sand, gravel, twigs, etc.
7. Secure the models to the base with glue.
8. Include a title and legend.
9. Draw a compass rose to orient the map.

Pilgrim Village
1627

1 Fort/ Meetinghouse
As the largest building, the fort was used for defense as well as a place of worship.

2 Standish Home Site
Captain Myles Standish was a veteran soldier. He became the colony's military commander.

3 Alden Home Site
John Alden worked as the Mayflower's cooper, or barrel-maker. He married another Mayflower passenger, Priscilla Mullins.

4 Bradford Home Site
William Bradford served as governor of the colony.

5 Hopkins Home Site
The son of Stephen Hopkins was born onboard the Mayflower during the crossing.

6 Howland Home Site
John Howland was a servant of the colony's first governor. He married Mayflower passenger Elizabeth Tilley who was orphaned the first winter.

7 Fuller Home Site
Samuel Fuller served as the colony's surgeon. His garden held a variety of medicinal herbs.

8 Annable Home Site
Anthony and Jane Annable arrived in New Plymouth with their two daughters in 1623.

9 Palmer Home Site
William Palmer was a nailer. His son arrived in 1621, and his wife joined them in 1623.

10 Storehouse
Community supplies were kept here as well as goods to be shipped to England in order to pay debts.

11 Forge
The colony's tools were made and maintained here by the village blacksmith.

12 Storehouse
This building served as an additional storage place for supplies and goods.

13 Browne Home Site
Peter Browne was one of the unmarried men who arrived on the Mayflower. He later married the widow Martha Ford.

14 Brewster Home Site
William Brewster held the office of Ruling Elder in the church at New Plymouth.

15 Billington Home Site
John Billington, Sr. was the first person to commit a punishable crime.

16 Allerton Home Site
Isaac Allerton married William Brewster's daughter, Fear.

17 Cooke Home Site
Francis Cooke arrived on the Mayflower with his son, John. His wife, Hester, followed in 1623 with the rest of the family.

18 Winslow Home Site
As an agent of the colony, Edward Winslow had made two voyages to England.

19 Beasthouse
Cattle and farm animals were kept in this small dwelling that opened into a grazing pasture.

20 Helm/Dutch Barn
This hay house is where the colonists stored their salt hay. It had an adjustable roof that could be raised or lowered depending on the supply of hay.

21 Oven
The colonists shared this communal oven where they would bake their breads and biscuits.

33

Geography-in-a-Box

ere's an eye-catching way for students to showcase their research skills. This project brings together note-taking and mapmaking as students research a state or country and present their findings in a shoe box. Students can draw or paint a state or national flag on the outside of the lid, and on the inside of the lid display a labeled map. The box itself can be used to hold items that represent the geography, history, and culture of the particular location. Items might include postcards, pictures, coins, stamps, an audiotape of a national anthem, and so on. An annotated inventory of the contents will help students sort their collections.

WHAT TO GET

- ➤ shoe box and lid
- ➤ glue
- ➤ brushes
- ➤ markers
- ➤ drawing paper
- ➤ acrylic paints
- ➤ pencils
- ➤ scissors

WHAT TO DO

1. Paint the outside box lid with a basecoat of white. Let it dry.
2. Use a pencil to draw the flag. Paint it and let it dry.
3. Paint the outside of the box. Let it dry.
4. Measure and cut drawing paper to fit the inside lid of the shoe box.
5. Draw a labeled map of the state, territory, or country. Color with markers or pencils.
6. Glue the map to the inside lid of the box.
7. Store all collected items in the box.

34

WRITING EXTENSION: Letters

When students have gathered information about a particular state or country, challenge them to write a letter as if they had traveled to that particular location. I make sure my students incorporate details that touch on at least five items they've included in their geography-in-a-box projects, as well as create a hand-drawn route map highlighting their travel itinerary. The letter is folded and enclosed in an envelope addressed to a friend or relative.

WRITING EXTENSION: Travel Brochure

Students design a travel brochure for their geography-in-a-box project that will lure readers to come and explore the featured place. One way students can make brochures is to fold large sheets of construction paper into three or four panels. Panels can then be sectioned to include maps, famous landmarks, information about currency and special events, and so forth. Consult actual brochures for layout ideas.

Book Link: Yildirim, Eljay. *Aunty Dot's Incredible Adventure Atlas.* New York: Reader's Digest Children's Publishing, 1997. As winners of the Jolly Sailor Tuna Contest, Dorothy and Frank Murphy set out on a trip around the world. Their sightseeing and adventures are chronicled in a series of letters, maps, and photo collages. Students will enjoy opening the attached air mail envelopes and reading Aunty Dot's letters, which are packed with fascinating information about her trip around the world. 📖

Web Link: Enchanted Learning—Geography
http://www.enchantedlearning.com/geography/
The easy to read text, printouts, and student activities makes this Web site an excellent source of information in planning the geobox contents. Click onto Japan, for example, and learn how to make an origami whale, read a Japanese folk tale, and listen to an audio clip of basic Japanese words. ☐

Web Link: Class Connect
http://www.gigglepotz.com/cc.htm
Click onto this Web site and join the Classroom Connect Program. Exchange geography-in-a-box projects with your E-pals from across the country or around the world. Your students will learn a great deal about their state or region as they research, plan, and assemble a local geography-in-a-box. They will love receiving one from their digital pen pals from England, Australia, or New Zealand. ☐

Web Link: Scholastic Classport
http://teacher.scholastic.com/activities/index.htm
Scholastic offers teachers a great opportunity to communicate and collaborate with classrooms from 182 countries. Register with Classport and partner with a classroom. Have your students become E-pals or share in an online project. Special features include a text translator as well as a clickable map that will access weather information all over the world. ☐

Map Checklist

	Yes	No
PLACES AND FEATURES		
All key places and natural features are included.	☐	☐
Places and features are correctly oriented according to north, south, east, and west.	☐	☐
Different political and/or physical areas are drawn in proportion to each other.	☐	☐
Coastlines and/or political boundaries are drawn accurately and with detail.	☐	☐
Colors are used to show differences in political or physical areas on the map.	☐	☐
LABELS		
All labels are included.	☐	☐
All labels are accurately placed.	☐	☐
All labels are spelled correctly.	☐	☐
All labels are easy to read.	☐	☐
MAP ELEMENTS		
The following are included:		
Title	☐	☐
Compass rose	☐	☐
Legend (if required)	☐	☐
Other (dates, scale, grid, direction arrows)	☐	☐

Map Rubric

	4 MASTER	3 PRACTITIONER	2 APPRENTICE	1 NOVICE
ACCURACY	➢ Map includes all relevant places and natural features. ➢ All places, features, and areas are correctly oriented and proportionately drawn. ➢ All coastlines and/or political borders are drawn with detail. ➢ All labels are included, accurately placed, and correctly spelled.	➢ Map includes most relevant places and natural features. ➢ Most places, features, and areas are correctly oriented and proportionately drawn. ➢ Most coastlines and/or political borders are drawn with detail. ➢ Most labels are included and most are accurately placed and correctly spelled.	➢ Map includes some relevant places and natural features. ➢ Some places, features, and areas are correctly oriented and proportionately drawn. ➢ Some coastlines and/or political borders are drawn with detail. ➢ Some labels are included, and some are accurately placed and correctly spelled.	➢ Map includes few relevant places and natural features. ➢ Few places, features, and areas are correctly oriented and proportionately drawn. ➢ Few coastlines and/or political borders are drawn with detail. ➢ Few labels are included and few are accurately placed and correctly spelled.
PRESENTATION	➢ Map is neatly drawn and well organized. ➢ Colors enhance the reading and appeal of the map. ➢ All labels are very easy to read.	➢ Map is neatly drawn and satisfactorily organized. ➢ Colors help make the map readable. ➢ Most labels are easy to read.	➢ Map is somewhat neat. ➢ Colors do not enhance organization or legibility. ➢ Some labels are easy to read.	➢ Map is carelessly drawn and lacks organization. ➢ Colors distract in the reading of the map. ➢ Few labels are easy to read.
USE OF MAP ELEMENTS	➢ Map includes all required elements. ➢ All map elements are used properly.	➢ Map includes most required elements. ➢ Most elements are used properly.	➢ Map includes some map elements. ➢ Some elements are used properly.	➢ Map includes few map elements. ➢ Few map elements are used properly.

Landform Terms Mini-Book and Activity Cards

Help students remember key landform terms with two easy-to-make activities that use the terms and definitions on pages 39–46. Students can create a Concentration-style card game or mini-reference book.

LANDFORM TERMS MINI-BOOK

Students can make their own mini-reference book to use during geography lessons and activities.

1. Make copies of pages 39–46 (one set per student).
2. Distribute the copies and have students:
   - Review terms and definitions.
   - Draw each landform above its name.
   - Make notes about the landform, such as where it can be found or how it was created.
   - Create additional pages for new terms using the blank template.
   - Cut apart the mini-book pages along the dotted lines so that each page contains a term and a definition.
   - Place the pages in alphabetical order.
   - Illustrate and place the Landform Terms cover page (page 39) on top.
   - Staple along the left edge to create a wide mini-book OR fold each page in half along the dashed lines and staple along the spine to create a tiny mini-book.

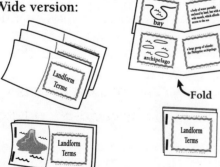

Wide version:

Tiny version:

Fold

MATCH IT! LANDFORM CARD GAME

This game helps students review the landform terms and definitions they've learned. You can add more definitions by making copies of and filling in the blank name and definition cards on page 46.

To make the card set:

1. On heavy stock paper, make copies of pages 39–46 (one set per pair or group of students).
2. Distribute the copies and have students:
   - Review terms and definitions
   - Draw each landform above its name.
   - Cut apart the cards along the dotted lines and the dashed lines, so that term cards are separate from definition cards.
   - Make an additional pair for the set using the blank name and definition cards. (Find an inventive way to use the Landform Terms card pair—perhaps as a bonus pair that counts as two pairs or as Skip-Your-Turn cards.)

To play:

1. Place all cards facedown on a desk or a table.
2. Roll a die to determine the playing order.
3. Players take turns flipping over two cards. If the cards match (the term matches the definition), the player wins that pair and takes another turn. If the cards do not match, the player turns them back over. The next player takes a turn, and so on. The game ends when all term-definition pairs have been correctly matched and collected. The player holding the most pairs wins. (Hint: The key to collecting the most pairs is remembering the location of cards that have been turned over.)

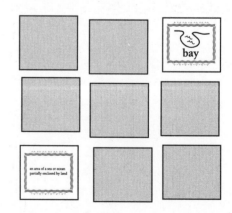

Landform Terms

archipelago

a group or chain of islands

bay

an area of a sea or ocean partially enclosed by land

beach

the shore of a body of water, especially when sandy or pebbly

butte

a hill that rises abruptly from the surrounding area and has sloping sides and a flat top

canyon

a deep valley with steep walls cut into the earth by running water

cape

a pointed landmass
projecting into a body
of water

continent

one of Earth's principal land
masses—Africa, Antarctica,
Asia, Australia, Europe,
North America, and South
America

delta

a usually triangular deposit
of silt at the mouth of a river

desert

a barren, often dry or
desolate area

gulf

a large area of a sea or ocean
partially enclosed by land

island

a landmass entirely
surrounded by water

isthmus

a narrow strip of land connecting two larger landmasses

lake

a large inland body of fresh water or salt water

mesa

a broad, flat-topped hill with steep sides

mountain

an elevation of Earth's surface with steep sides and a height greater than that of a hill

ocean

the entire body of salt water that covers more than 70 percent of Earth's surface

peninsula

a landmass that is surrounded by water on three sides

plateau

an elevated, flat landmass

river

a large natural stream of water emptying into an ocean, a lake, or another body of water

sea

a large body of salt water completely or partially enclosed by land

strait

a narrow body of water joining two larger bodies of water

volcano

an opening in Earth's crust through which molten lava, ash, and gases are ejected

_____

_____
_____
_____
_____

Great Geography Bibliography: Books and Web Sites

The following reference books and Web sites provide a wealth of geographic information as well as excellent maps that students can consult as they make and label their own maps. Add them to your library shelves and bookmark favorite sites on your computer!

Atlases

Lye, Keith, and Alistair Campbell. *Atlas in the Round: Our Planet as You've Never Seen It.* Philadelphia: Running Press, 1999.
> This unique atlas views Earth as seen from space. Its spherical maps provide a more accurate representation of the world than flat maps. Information about each of the continents and oceans is presented with simple text and accompanied by captioned pictures.

National Geographic United States Atlas for Young Explorers. Washington, D.C.: National Geographic Society, 1999.
> This collection of state, regional, and national maps provides a complete reference to the United States. Each state has a double-page spread packed with vital facts and figures.

National Geographic World Atlas for Young Explorers. Washington, D.C.: National Geographic Society, 1998.
> Each map is generously presented over two pages, and the accompanying text is interesting and easy to read. Thematic maps on world population, environment, and endangered species, as well as stunning photographs, make this book an invaluable reference for the young geographer.

Rand McNally Around the World: Atlas of Maps and Pictures. Skokie, IL: Rand McNally, 1994.
> This collection of maps is organized by continent, and the simple text is very easy to read. Each map is bordered with colorful illustrations of interesting facts, such as local foods and customs. Many of the pictures portray local children at work or play.

Reader's Digest Children's Atlas of the World. Pleasantville, N.Y.: Reader's Digest Children's Publishing, 1998.
> Updated for the new millennium, this atlas is chock-full of interesting facts that will intrigue readers. Many of the country maps offer suggested activities that provide hands-on geography as well as extend learning beyond the covers of this book.

Series

Dorling Kindersley Eyewitness Series
> These graphically rich books are very appealing to readers of all ages. Titles include *Africa, Arctic and Antarctica, Desert, Russia, Bible Lands, Ancient China, Ancient Egypt, Ancient Greece*, and *Ancient Rome*.

Fradin, Dennis Brindell. From Sea to Shining Sea Series. Danbury, CT: Children's Press.
> This series of state books presents a wealth of information about each state's geography, history, and people. Each book contains labeled maps as well as color photographs. The easy-to-read prose makes information accessible to many readers.

Heinrichs, Ann. Enchantment of the World Series. Danbury, CT: Children's Press.
> The titles in this series include *Australia, Brazil, Egypt, Japan, Nepal, Tibet*, and soon-to-be-published *Niger*. Each book is written with easy-to-read prose filled with information that will appeal to children. The abundance of color photographs makes these books a great visual introduction to the geography, history, and culture of these countries.

Reynolds, Jan. Vanishing Cultures Series. Orlando, FL: Harcourt Brace.
> Seven books make up this photoessay series that deals with indigenous peoples. They are *Sahara, Himalaya, Amazon Basin, Frozen Lands, Down Under, Mongolia,* and *Far North*. The simple and informative text is accompanied by color photographs depicting scenes of the daily life of these cultures.

Web Links

A to Z Geography
http://school.discovery.com/homeworkhelp/worldbook/atozgeography/
The alphabetical organization of this site makes finding information about cities, countries, and regions very easy. Just click on to any letter of the alphabet, and articles and maps focusing on Aachen, Germany, to Zurich, Switzerland, will be made available.

Atlapedia Online
http://www.atlapedia.com/index.html
This digital atlas provides full-color physical and political maps of major countries—from Afghanistan to Zimbabwe.

Color Landform Atlas of the United States
http://fermi.jhuapl.edu/states/states.html
An alphabetical listing of states provides all sorts of maps. Come here to find shaded and black-and-white relief maps, county maps, and satellite images from Alabama to Wyoming.

Evergreen Project
http://mbgnet.mobot.org/
This site focuses on Earth's different biomes and ecosystems. Find out what life is like in the rain forest, tundra, taiga, desert, temperate, and grasslands regions. Learn about creatures that live in freshwater and marine ecosystems.

Geo-Globe
http://library.thinkquest.org/10157/geoglobe.html
This geography site is organized into six interactive sections. Through games and quizzes students will have fun as they learn a great deal about the world.

Geography
http://www.geography.about.com
This Web site is an extensive geographic resource. Printable outline maps of the world, individual countries, and U.S. states are available for use in the classroom. Clicks on the navigation bar will lead you to great geography lesson plans, games, and much more.

Greatest Places On Line
http://www.greatestplaces.org/
Are you looking for information on the Amazon, Greenland, Iguazú Falls, Madagascar, Namibia, Okavango, or Tibet? Read about their people and geography. An audio clip or a short video will take you to these fascinating places.

How Far Is It?
http://www.indo.com/distance/
If you need to calculate the distance between two places, you've come to the right Web site. Type in the requested information in the pop-up boxes, and you'll soon have the answer. A map showing the two locations is also provided.

Maps.com
http://maps.com/
The Explore With Maps channel on this Web site features an online atlas, a dynamic U.S. map, a world fact book, and games. Play a round of ALIENZ as you beam space creatures to different locations on a world map.

MegaMaps
http://www.yourchildlearns.com/megamaps.htm
Use your computer to print out a map of the United States or the world. Maps can range from a single page map to 64 pages. When pieced together, these large outline maps can be almost seven feet long!

National Geographic
http://www.nationalgeographic.com
Maps, maps, and more maps are featured at this premier geography site. Interactive adventures, an atlas of over 1,800 printable maps, and magazine articles are just a few of its features.

Postcards From America
http://postcardsfrom.com/
Trek the information highway and see America via electronic postcards. The postcards feature photographs, graphics, and information about significant sites within a 100-mile radius of the state capital.

States and Capitals
http://50states.com/
If you need information about the United States, this is the site to visit. Clicking on to any of the states on this site's alphabetical listing will reap a wealth of geographical and historical data. From maps of counties to images of license plates, you'll find whatever you are looking for and much more.

United Nations Cyberschool Bus
http://www.un.org/Pubs/CyberSchoolBus/index.html
Click on to InfoNation or Country at a Glance for information about member countries of the UN. Play Flag Tag, track the professor's whereabouts in Professor's Postcards, or test your geography knowledge in Quick Questions.